GAO Highlights

Accountability * Integrity * Reliability

Highlights of GAO-11-891, a report to congressional addressees

CONTINGENCY CONTRACTING

Improved Planning and Management Oversight Needed to Address Challenges with Closing Contracts

I0409637

Why GAO Did This Study

Since 2002, DOD obligated at least $166.6 billion on contracts supporting reconstruction and stabilization efforts in Iraq and Afghanistan. Many of these contingency contracts, in particular those awarded in Iraq, need to be closed. Contract closeout is a key step to ensure the government receives the goods and services it purchased at the agreed upon price and, if done timely, provides opportunities to use unspent funds for other needs and reduces exposure to other financial risks.

To assess DOD's efforts to close its Iraq contracts, GAO examined the (1) number of contracts that are eligible for closeout and the extent to which they will be closed within required time frames, (2) factors contributing to contracts not being closed within required time frames, (3) steps DOD took to manage the financial risks associated with not closing contracts within required time frames, and (4) extent to which DOD captured and implemented lessons learned from closing its Iraq contracts. GAO reviewed contingency contracting guidance, analyzed contract and closeout data for contracts awarded between fiscal years 2003 and 2010, and interviewed DOD officials from six organizations responsible for awarding or closing out these contracts.

What GAO Recommends

GAO is making three recommendations to ensure DOD has sufficient resources to close its Iraq and Afghanistan contracts and to better plan for and improve visibility of closeout efforts in future contingencies. DOD concurred with each of the recommendations.

View GAO-11-891 for key components. For more information, contact John P. Hutton at (202) 512-4841 or huttonj@gao.gov.

What GAO Found

DOD does not have visibility into the number of its Iraq contracts eligible for closeout, but available data indicate that DOD must still review and potentially close at least 58,000 contracts awarded between fiscal years 2003 and 2010. GAO's analysis indicates that relatively few of its contracts will be closed within required time frames. For example, about 90 percent of the limited number of contracts for which DOD could provide closeout data are already over age for closeout. The U.S. Central Command's Contracting Command (C3) and its predecessors, which awarded many of DOD's Iraq contracts, did not have sufficient internal controls to ensure that contracting data were accurate and complete. C3's management visibility was further affected by limitations of its information systems, staff turnover, and poor contract administration.

DOD's ability to close its contracts has been hindered by the lack of advance planning, workforce shortfalls, and contractor accounting challenges. For example, DOD's contingency contracting doctrine and guidance do not specifically require advanced planning for contract closeouts. DOD took steps in 2008 to address its backlog of contracts needing to be closed but such actions came too late to make significant difference in closing contracts within required time frames. DOD is now transitioning responsibility for closing out C3's contracts to the Army Contracting Command. Staffing challenges, however, during this transition have hindered efforts to close these contracts. Efforts to close large, cost-type contracts have been further hindered by Defense Contract Audit Agency staffing shortages and unresolved issues with contractors' accounting practices, which have delayed audits of the contractors' incurred costs.

DOD's efforts to identify unspent contract funds and improper payments—two examples of financial risks that timely closeout of contracts may help identify—are hindered by limited visibility into its Iraq contracts. DOD identified at least $135 million in unspent funds that could potentially not be available to meet other DOD needs. If not used, these funds will be returned to the U.S. Treasury at the end of fiscal year 2011. Should DOD identify a need to pay for an unanticipated cost on these contracts, it will need to use other funds that are currently available. Additionally, instances of improper payments and potential fraud were sometimes found years after final contract deliveries were made, making it harder for DOD to recover funds owed to it and increasing the risk that it may need to pay contractors interest fees on late payments.

DOD has identified and addressed some of the problems related to the closeout of Iraq contracts, but the growing backlog of over 42,000 Afghanistan contracts that need to be closed suggests the underlying causes have not been resolved. DOD officials noted that the lessons learned in Iraq highlight the need to improve contract data, increase the emphasis on contract administration and closeout, and improve contingency contracting doctrine and guidance. DOD officials reported that actions are underway to correct these deficiencies in future contingencies, but fully implementing these initiatives may take several years.

Contents

Figures

Abbreviations

ACC-RI	Army Contract Command-Rock Island
AFCEE	Air Force Center for Engineering and the Environment
C3	U.S. Central Command Contracting Command
DCAA	Defense Contract Audit Agency
DCMA	Defense Contract Management Agency
DFAS	Defense Finance and Accounting Service
DOD	Department of Defense
FAR	Federal Acquisition Regulation
LOGCAP	Logistics Civil Augmentation Program
USACE	U.S. Army Corps of Engineers

United States Government Accountability Office
Washington, DC 20548

September 27, 2011

Congressional Addressees

Since 2002, the Department of Defense (DOD) has reported obligations of at least $166.6 billion to acquire goods and services needed to support its reconstruction and stabilization efforts in Iraq and Afghanistan, according to the Commission on Wartime Contracting. Our work, as well as that of others, has documented shortcomings in DOD's strategic planning for operational contract support, contract administration and oversight, and its acquisition workforce in these contingency operations. Many of the contracts that were awarded to support these efforts have been completed and must be closed as the final step in the acquisition process. Contract closeout includes a number of administrative actions, including DOD confirming that all goods and services were received and issuing final payment to the contractor, the contractor acknowledging that the U.S. government does not owe it additional payment, and finally, the government deobligating any unspent funds. For contracts awarded on a cost-reimbursable basis, the Defense Contract Audit Agency (DCAA) conducts audits to assist the contracting officer in determining that contractor costs are allowable, allocable, and reasonable.

The Federal Acquisition Regulation (FAR) states that firm-fixed price contracts should be closed within 6 months after the contract is physically completed, which generally occurs when the government accepts final delivery of goods and services.[1] Cost-type contracts should be closed within 36 months and can be more difficult to close than firm-fixed price contracts as they require the settlement of indirect cost rates.[2] Closing contracts within these time frames can help to limit the government's exposure to certain financial risks by identifying and recovering improper payments and avoiding paying interest fees when the government does not pay contractors on time. Timely closeout also ensures that DOD deobligates and uses unspent funds from completed contracts before the

---

[1] FAR § 4.804-1(a)(2).

[2] FAR § 4.804-1(a)(3).

GAO-11-891 Contingency Contracting

funds are canceled and return to the U.S. Department of the Treasury (Treasury).[3] The timing for when funds are canceled is set by statute.

Many DOD organizations awarded contracts to support military operations in Iraq, but the majority in our review were awarded in theater by U.S. Central Command's Contracting Command (C3) and its predecessor organizations.[4] In 2007, the Gansler Commission on Army Acquisition and Program Management in Expeditionary Operations found that only 5 percent of Iraq contracts were being closed. In response to these findings, the Army established a Contract Closeout Task Force Office (Task Force) to close C3's Iraq and Afghanistan firm-fixed price contracts and estimated its mission would be completed in January 2011. C3, however, significantly underestimated the total number of contracts it needed to close and is now transferring the Task Force's mission to Army Contract Command-Rock Island (ACC-RI). ACC-RI is also responsible for managing the Army's Logistics Civil Augmentation Program (LOGCAP) contracts. C3 has also delegated closeout responsibilities of its cost-type contracts to the Defense Contract Management Agency (DCMA) Southern Europe. Additionally, U.S. Army Corps of Engineers (USACE) and Air Force's Center for Engineering and the Environment (AFCEE) also awarded many Iraq contracts but generally retained responsibility for closing those contracts.

To assess DOD's efforts to close its Iraq contracts, under the authority of the Comptroller General to conduct evaluations on his own initiative to assist Congress with its oversight responsibilities, we examined the (1) total number of its contracts with performance in Iraq that are eligible for closeout and the extent to which DOD closed these contracts within required time frames, (2) factors that contributed to contracts not being closed within required time frames, (3) steps DOD took to manage the financial risks associated with not closing contracts within required time

---

[3] For appropriated funds, Congress specifies the period of time each appropriation can be used. Any funds not obligated within their period of availability are considered expired. Expired funds cannot be used for new obligations but can be used up to 5 years after they expire to pay for authorized increases to existing obligations made from the same appropriation. Any funds remaining after the 5-year period are considered canceled and must be returned to the Treasury.

[4] C3 became the Joint Theater Support Contracting Command for Iraq and Afghanistan on June 11, 2010. C3 was preceded by the Joint Contracting Command – Iraq/Afghanistan, the Project and Contracting Office, and the Coalition Provisional Authority.

frames, and (4) extent to which DOD captured and implemented lessons learned from closing its Iraq contracts.

To determine the number of DOD's Iraq contracts eligible for closeout and the extent to which DOD closed these contracts within required time frames, we reviewed the FAR and the Defense Federal Acquisition Regulation Supplement to determine when a contract is eligible for closeout and the time frames and the procedures for closing contracts. For the purpose of our review the term contracts refers to all base contracts, task orders, and blanket purchase agreement call orders. We obtained contract data from four DOD organizations that our prior work indicated had been responsible for awarding many of the contracts with performance in Iraq: C3, Army's ACC-RI, USACE, and AFCEE. These organizations may retain responsibility for administering and closing the contracts they awarded, or they may delegate such responsibilities to another organization. In those instances, we obtained contract data from that organization. From each organization, we requested the contract number, period of performance, contract type, contract status, total obligations, total unliquidated obligations, and physical completion dates for each contract for which they were responsible to close. The data we obtained from the Task Force also included contracts with performance in Afghanistan, which we identified separately in our analysis. In instances in which DOD did not have complete data, we used available data to determine the number of contracts eligible for closeout. We assessed the reliability of these data reported by the contracting organizations through interviews with knowledgeable officials and electronic data testing for missing data, outliers, and obvious errors within each database. While we found that C3's contract data from fiscal years 2003 through 2008 were generally unreliable for determining the closeout status of contracts, they were sufficiently reliable for determining the minimum number of contracts awarded during this time period. We did not assess the reliability of the financial management systems used by DOD to provide financial data for our review.

To identify the factors that contributed to contracts not being closed within required time frames, we reviewed DOD's closeout planning documents and interviewed officials at each of the contracting organizations, DCAA, and the Defense Finance and Accounting Service (DFAS), which is responsible for making payments on many Iraq contracts, and U.S. Army Central. We reviewed DOD's policy and guidance to determine how contract closeout should be incorporated into contingency contracting planning. To understand any challenges faced by DOD contracting personnel in closing individual contracts, we reviewed contract documents for 25 firm-fixed price contracts purposefully selected to obtain a variety of closeout organizations and a range of closeout difficulty and interviewed contracting personnel on their experiences with closing them. We also reviewed the Task Force's and ACC-RI's monthly closeout data to assess the Army's progress in closing C3's contracts. In addition, to identify the factors that affected the completion of audits of cost-type contracts, we purposefully selected eight contractors based on the number of over-age task orders, the amount obligated on the contract, and the amount of unliquidated obligations. We reviewed completed audit reports and interviewed DCAA officials at headquarters and eight field offices to determine what factors affected their ability to complete planned audits associated with those contractors.

To determine the steps DOD has taken to manage the financial risks associated with closing contracts, we reviewed the DOD Financial Management Regulation and closeout guidance and interviewed contracting and financial management personnel at the Office of the Under Secretary of Defense, Comptroller; Office of the Assistant Secretary of the Army, Financial Management & Comptroller; Joint Chiefs of Staff Force Structure, Resources, and Assessment Directorate (J-8); and USACE Resource Management. In addition, we analyzed unliquidated obligation data and interviewed contracting and financial management personnel at each contracting organization we met with to determine how these funds were managed and if any funds would be returned to Treasury. We also reviewed contracts with known improper payments and interviewed DFAS personnel to assess DOD's ability to recover such payments.

To assess the extent to which DOD captured and implemented lessons learned from closing contracts in contingency operations, we interviewed contracting officials at each of the organizations we visited and reviewed C3 documents on contracting-related problems encountered in Iraq. We also interviewed senior contracting officials in Iraq and Afghanistan to identify any changes made in response to the lessons learned from closing the C3 contracts. We obtained and reviewed C3 data on the total number of contracts in Afghanistan that are eligible and over age for closeout to assess its progress in closing these contracts. We also interviewed Army, Joint Chiefs of Staff, and Acquisition, Technology, and Logistics' Office of Defense Procurement and Acquisition Policy officials responsible for setting policy and issuing guidance to identify changes made to respond to the problems encountered in Iraq. See appendix I for additional details on our scope and methodology.

We conducted this performance audit from July 2010 through September 2011 in accordance with generally accepted government auditing standards. Those standards require that we plan and perform the audit to obtain sufficient, appropriate evidence to provide a reasonable basis for our findings and conclusions based on our audit objectives. We believe that the evidence obtained provides a reasonable basis for our findings and conclusions based on our audit objectives

Background

DOD faces a number of long-standing and systemic challenges that have hindered its ability to achieve more successful acquisition outcomes, such as ensuring that DOD personnel use sound contracting approaches and maintaining a workforce with the skills and capabilities needed to properly manage the acquisitions and oversee contractors. While the issues encountered in Iraq and Afghanistan are emblematic of these systemic challenges, their significance and effect are heightened in a contingency environment.[5] For example, in 2004, we raised concerns about DOD's ability to effectively administer and oversee contracts in Iraq, in part because of the continued expansion of reconstruction efforts, staffing constraints, and the need to operate in an unsecure and threatening environment.[6] Similarly, we reported in July 2007 that DOD had not completed negotiations on certain task orders in Iraq until more than 6 months after the work began and after most of the costs had been incurred, contributing to its decision to pay the contractor nearly all of the $221 million questioned by auditors.[7] In 2008, we reported that not having qualified personnel hindered oversight of contracts to maintain military equipment in Kuwait and provide linguistic services in Iraq and questioned whether DOD could sustain increased oversight of its private security contractors.[8]

---

[5] GAO, *Contingency Contracting: Observations on Actions Needed to Address Systemic Challenges*, GAO-11-580 (Washington, D.C.: Apr. 25, 2011).

[6] GAO, *Rebuilding Iraq: Fiscal Year 2003 Contract Award Procedures and Management Challenges*, GAO-04-605 (Washington, D.C.: June 1, 2004).

[7] GAO, *Defense Contract Management: DOD's Lack of Adherence to Key Contracting Principles on Iraq Oil Contract Put Government Interests at Risk*, GAO-07-839 (Washington, D.C.: July 31, 2007).

[8] GAO, *Military Operations: DOD Needs to Address Contract Oversight and Quality Assurance Issues for Contracts Used to Support Contingency Operations*, GAO-08-1087 (Washington, D.C.: Sept. 26, 2008).

The contract closeout process includes verifying that the goods or services were provided and that all final administrative steps are completed, including an audit of the costs billed to the government and adjusting for any over- or underpayments on the final invoice. To close a contract, DOD must complete a number of tasks, including making final payment to the contractor, receiving a release of claims from the contractor, and deobligating excess funds, among other tasks (see fig. 1). A contract is eligible to be closed once the contract is physically complete, which is generally when all option provisions have expired and the contractor has completed performance and the government has accepted the final delivery of goods or services in the form of a receiving report or the government has provided the contractor a notice of complete contract termination.[9] From this point, contracts should be closed within time frames set by the FAR—6 months for firm-fixed price contracts and 36 months for cost-type contracts and time and materials contracts. Additional time is allowed for the closeout of these latter contract types as the contracting officer and DCAA may need to ensure any incurred costs are allowable, allocable, and reasonable. Additional time is also needed to set the final indirect overhead rates, which determine, in part the contractor's final payment on cost-type contracts.[10] When the contract completion statement, also known as the DD 1594, is signed by the contracting officer, the contract is considered closed and contract documents can be stored and retained.

---

[9] Files for contracts using simplified acquisition procedures should be considered closed when the contracting officer receives evidence of receipt of property and final payment, unless otherwise specified by agency regulations. FAR § 4.804-1(a)(1).

[10] The FAR also prohibits the closing of contract files if the contract is in litigation, under appeal, or where the contract is being terminated and all termination actions have not been completed. FAR § § 4.804-1(c)(1) and (2).

Figure 1: Overview of Contract Closeout Process

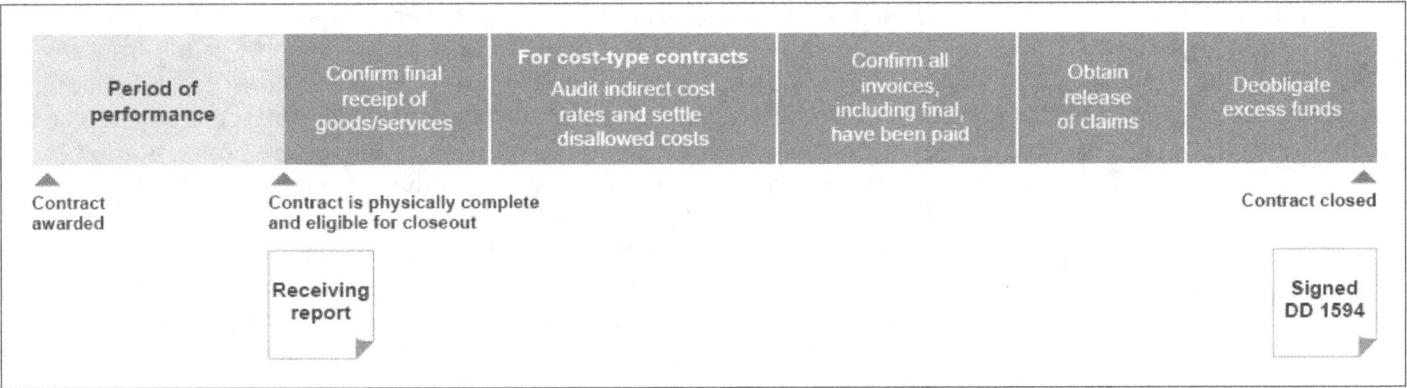

Source: GAO analysis of the Federal Acquisition Regulation and DOD guidance on contract closeouts.

A contract not closed within the FAR time frames is considered to be over age for closeout and increases an organization's exposure to a number of financial issues. If contract closeout does not take place in a timely manner and funds are not deobligated when currently available, the agency loses the use of those funds for new obligations. Even if funds are expired when they are deobligated, the agency can still use them for up to 5 years after they expire to pay for authorized increases to existing obligations made from the same appropriation. Any funds remaining after the 5-year period are considered canceled and must be returned to Treasury. If closeout does not take place until after they are canceled, and the agency identifies a need for the government to pay the contractor for an unanticipated cost, the government must use other funds that are currently available. Additionally, the risk of late payments to contractors increases when contracts are not closed within required time frames and in turn may result in the government paying interest. Further, the longer an organization waits to close a contract the more difficult it becomes to identify and recover improper payments to contractors. In addition, closing a contract years after the performance is complete can be more time consuming because key documentation, such as invoices and receiving reports, and contracting personnel with first-hand knowledge of the contract may no longer be available.

DOD's Visibility into the Number of Contracts Eligible for Closeout Is Hindered by Inadequate Data

DOD does not have visibility into the total number of its Iraq contracts eligible for closeout, but our analysis of available data indicates that relatively few of these contracts will be closed within the time frames prescribed by the FAR. C3, which awarded the majority of the Iraq contracts, did not have sufficient internal controls to ensure its contracting data were accurate and complete, and was further affected by limitations of its contracting systems, turnover in contracting personnel, and other competing demands. In 2009, to help reduce the backlog of contracts to be closed, C3 transferred 66,760 Iraq contracts and 14,336 contracts in which a place of performance was not specified to the Task Force.[11] As it was unclear how many of these contracts were closed before being shipped, Task Force personnel are in the process of reviewing each contract and, as appropriate, closing any open contracts. As of April 2011, however, over 54,000 of these contracts still needed to be reviewed. DOD officials noted that record keeping generally improved for C3's firm-fixed price contracts awarded after fiscal year 2008. C3 also improved visibility of its large, cost-type contracts awarded between fiscal year 2003 and 2010 after delegating contract administration, including closeout responsibilities, to DCMA Southern Europe in 2008. Based on available data provided by C3 and the other DOD contracting organizations we reviewed, there are at least an additional 4,298 Iraq contracts—90 percent of which are already over age—that need to be closed.

C3's Visibility into Its Contracting Activity Improved in Fiscal Year 2009 but Reliability of Prior Years' Data Is Questionable

C3 and its predecessor organizations awarded the majority of DOD's contracts to support reconstruction and stabilization efforts, yet weak internal controls, turnover in contracting personnel, and competing demands contributed to incomplete or inaccurate information that hindered management oversight of its contracting activities, including whether it was meeting FAR closeout requirements.[12] DOD officials noted C3 did not have a contract writing and management information system in Iraq between 2003 and 2008, which contributed to the use of multiple

---

[11] C3 data reported a total of seven fiscal year 2002 contracts awarded before operations began in Iraq that we found to be coded incorrectly.

[12] Internal controls should provide reasonable assurance that the objectives of the agency are being achieved in the following categories: effectiveness and efficiency of operations including the use of the entity's resources; reliability of financial reporting, including reports on budget execution, financial statements, and other reports for internal and external use; and compliance with applicable laws and regulations. GAO/AIMD-00-21.3.1

manual databases. Each regional contracting center awarded manually written contracts and documented contract actions on independent spreadsheets. C3 and Army officials noted some of the challenges with manually written contracts included duplicate or inaccurate contract numbers and inaccurate period of performance dates. They also noted that each regional contracting center maintained and managed its contract data on spreadsheets differently as there was not an Iraq-wide standard for how to maintain contract data and that data input was often unverified. These contract documentation challenges were exacerbated by the constant turnover of contracting personnel and the command's emphasis on awarding contracts to support the warfighter. Additionally, C3 and Army officials said that an unknown number of contracts were never input into C3's database and could not be accounted for because contract files were lost, damaged, or destroyed.

Our analysis of C3's data on its Iraq contracts found at least 55,000 contracts were recorded as being awarded between fiscal years 2003 and 2008, but we determined that the data had numerous discrepancies. These discrepancies, which included missing or invalid period of performance and physical completion dates as well as invalid or duplicative contract numbers, affect the data needed to maintain visibility on the contracts eligible to be closed. Army officials acknowledged that the contract information reflected in C3's database through fiscal year 2008 was unreliable for determining the actual number of contracts it awarded or which contracts were eligible to be closed. Consequently, the Army underestimated the total number of contracts that the Task Force needed to close. In 2008, the Army estimated that the Task Force would need to close approximately 24,000 contracts awarded by C3 in Iraq and Afghanistan from 2003 to 2008, but the Task Force recorded that C3 sent it 103,693 contracts (see table 1). Our analysis of the Task Force's data indicates that C3 transferred at least 66,760 Iraq contracts, including approximately 8,500 more contracts awarded between fiscal years 2003 and 2008 than what was reflected in C3's database. Additionally, the Task Force inventoried another 14,336 contracts for which the place of performance was not specified.[13] Army officials stated that C3 had closed some of these contracts before sending the files to the Task Force, but acknowledged that the C3 data did not accurately reflect which contracts

---

[13] C3 also transferred 22,597 of its Afghanistan contracts that were awarded between 2002 and 2008 to the Task Force to be reviewed and closed.

were closed. Therefore, the Army required Task Force personnel to review each contract and close those that remain open. Army officials stated, however, that there have been no attempts to reconcile the C3 contracting data with the Task Force's findings.

Table 1: Status of C3 Contracts Inventoried and Reviewed by the Task Force as of April 2011

Place of contract performance	Reviewed	Not reviewed	Total contracts inventoried
Iraq	26,735	40,025	**66,760**
Not specified[a]	—	14,336	**14,336**
Afghanistan	3,510	19,087	**22,597**
Total	**30,245**[b]	**73,448**	**103,693**[c]

Source: GAO analysis of DOD data.

[a]DOD generally uses a DOD Activity Address Code within the contract identification number to identify the office awarding the contract. According to C3's Acquisition Instruction, these contracts reflected Activity Address Codes that were not among those C3 personnel were authorized to use in Iraq and Afghanistan. We were unable to identify the place of performance for these contracts because there was no such data available in the Task Force's database as these contracts have not yet been reviewed for closeout.

[b]GAO analysis indicates that 30,048 contracts were reviewed and closed, as appropriate, by Task Force personnel. There were an additional 129 contracts under review, but not closed, and another 68 contracts under review with a place of performance other than Iraq or Afghanistan.

[c]Nearly all of the contracts sent to the Task Force were awarded from fiscal year 2002 to 2008. Task Force data, however, also indicate that 3,165 Iraq contracts, 2,964 Afghanistan contracts, and 2 unspecified contracts awarded between fiscal years 2009 and 2010 were sent to the Task Force. We could not determine the award year for another 287 contracts.

The extent to which the contracts that have not yet been reviewed by Task Force personnel and will need to be closed is uncertain, in part, because some that were reportedly closed by C3 still required contract administration. For example, Task Force personnel stated that contracts sometimes included a signed DD 1594 even though the contracts still required administrative actions.

To improve the management of its contracts, C3 began using the Standard Procurement System in fiscal year 2009. Both Army and C3 officials stated that the Standard Procurement System had better quality control checks to generate valid contract numbers with automated prompts requiring contracting personnel to insert required data fields, such as period of performance, at the time of award. These officials also said that the quality control checks improved the completeness and quality of C3's data and provided better insight needed to manage the contract closeout process. Army officials said that once the Standard

Procurement System was deployed in Iraq, the regional contracting centers were able to transmit data back to Army locations in the United States which could be used to run automated reports on contracts closed, eligible for closeout, and over age for closeout. Army and C3 officials acknowledged that while the data improved, C3 continued to identify problems with the data input by contracting personnel. In a July 2010 memorandum, C3 directed its personnel to take actions to improve the overall quality, accuracy, and timelines of C3's contracting actions. For example, it identified specific data fields, including those that help to determine a contract's eligibility for closeout, that personnel are required to capture in C3's data systems.

C3 obtained better visibility of its firm-fixed price contracts awarded in fiscal years 2009 and later as well as their large, cost-type contracts. C3's data on these firm-fixed price contracts indicates that C3 closed over 9,600 of its Iraq contracts awarded between fiscal years 2009 and 2010. Similarly, DOD officials indicated that C3 had better visibility of its large, cost-type contracts awarded between fiscal years 2003 and 2010, in part because it generally delegated contract administration for these contracts, including closeout responsibilities, to DCMA Southern Europe in 2008. DCMA officials reported that when it accepted C3's cost-type contracts, the files were in generally poor condition and missing documents. DCMA officials reported, however, that they devoted the resources necessary to collect missing information for these contracts and developed their own data to manage the closeout of these contracts and task orders. Our analysis of these firm-fixed price and cost-type contracts indicates that 97 percent were over age as of May 2011 (see table 2).

Table 2: Closeout Status for Selected C3 Contracts as of May 2011

Fiscal year awarded	Contract type	Eligible to close	Over age	Percent over age
2009-2010	Firm-fixed price	3,282	3,192	97
2003-2010	Cost-type	109	106	97
Total		**3,391**	**3,298**	**97**

Source: GAO analysis of DOD data.

Other DOD Organizations Had Better Visibility of Contracts, but Challenges Remain for Closeout

ACC-RI, AFCEE, and USACE officials indicated that the use of existing contracting systems at the onset of military operations in Iraq provided them better visibility into the number of contracts they had awarded to support efforts in Iraq. Agency officials acknowledged, however, that they sometimes encountered challenges with using their existing systems. For example, USACE officials noted that the standard reports used to determine which Iraq contracts needed to be closed were initially inaccurate because period of performance or physical completion dates were not correctly entered into their contracting systems. As a result, USACE officials found in March 2011 that USACE's closeout reports underestimated the number of contracts eligible and over age for closeout due to inaccurate period of performance dates. USACE revised its reports using period of performance dates from other data sources, which identified that 639 contracts were eligible to be closed, more than 300 contracts than its initial report reflected. Similarly, AFCEE's data indicate that the period of performance ended for 154 of its Iraq contracts but the data did not reflect whether final goods and services had been delivered and whether the contract was physically complete. Our analysis indicates that the period of performance ended at least 3 years ago for 37 of these contracts, but AFCEE personnel stated that they cannot close these contracts until they receive final documentation that the goods and services have been delivered. Overall, we estimate that about 66 percent of these organizations' 907 eligible contracts are over age (see table 3).

Table 3: DOD Iraq Contracts Reported Eligible and Over Age for Closeout

Contracting organization	Contract type	Eligible to close	Over age	Percent over age
ACC-RI LOGCAP	Cost-type	18	17	94
AFCEE	Firm-fixed price	5	4	80
	Cost-type	222	83	37
	Time and materials	23	9	39
USACE	Firm-fixed price	572	463	81
	Cost-type	63	20	32
	Time and materials	4	0	0
Total		**907**	**596**	**66**

Source: GAO analysis of data reported by contracting organizations between January and June 2011.

Our analysis of data provided by these contracting organizations reflects a higher percent of eligible firm-fixed price contracts that are over age compared to eligible cost-type contracts, in part due to the longer period of time allowed by the FAR to close out cost-type contracts.[14] For

---

[14] FAR § § 4.804-1(a)(2) and (3).

GAO-11-891 Contingency Contracting

example, our analysis indicates that about 81 percent of the firm-fixed price contracts eligible to be closed were over age compared to approximately 40 percent of eligible cost-type contracts. Nevertheless, these organizations have closed few of their cost-type Iraq contracts. For example, USACE data indicate that it had closed 7 of its 77 Iraq cost-type contracts and AFCEE had closed just 10 of its 239 Iraq cost-type contracts awarded since 2003.

Planning, Workforce, and Contractor Accounting Issues Hinder Efforts to Close Contracts

DOD's ability to close the contracts it awarded to support efforts in Iraq is hindered by several factors, including the failure to plan for or emphasize the need to close these contracts until reconstruction efforts were well underway, staffing shortfalls, and contractor accounting issues. DOD did not plan for or focus on closing its Iraq contracts until 2008, in part because DOD's contingency contracting policy and guidance do not emphasize the need to plan for contract closeouts during the early stages of a contingency operation. DOD has taken steps to reduce the number of firm-fixed price contracts it needs to close, but ACC-RI has not been able to hire enough personnel to replace Task Force personnel during the transition of closeout responsibilities, which has slowed these efforts. Similarly, efforts to close its large, cost-type contracts is hindered by staffing shortages at DCAA and unresolved issues with contractors' cost accounting practices that preclude completing the necessary audits of the contractors' incurred costs. As a result, DOD is unlikely to close 226 cost-type contracts with over $19.1 billion in obligations in the near future.

DOD Doctrine and Policy Do Not Emphasize Advanced Planning for Closeout

DOD contingency contracting doctrine and policy do not specifically include closeout as part of the advanced planning for a contingency operation. Since 2006, a contract support integration plan annex termed Annex W—which provide details on the contractor support required during a contingency, including the military's organizational requirements needed to acquire and oversee such support—has been required to be in

DOD's most detailed operation plans.[15] In October 2008, DOD established its first doctrine to standardize guidance for planning, conducting, and assessing operational contract support integration, contractor management functions, and contracting command and control in support of joint operations in its Joint Publication 4-10, *Operational Contract Support*.[16] In part, this doctrine provides guidance for contingency contracting requirements that should be planned for within the Annex W. While it states that an Annex W should outline all activities necessary to execute contract support integration requirements in an operational area, it does not specifically direct DOD commands to determine an approach for closing contracts in advance or even during the initial stages of a contingency operation. Joint Publication 4-10 advises that contracts be closed as performance is completed, consistent with the requirements established in the FAR, but makes no reference for the need to plan for the resources needed to close contracts within required time frames. Instead, contract closeout is described as part of the redeployment and contract termination phase, the fourth and final operational phase of a contingency. In 2009, DOD issued a template for planners to use when developing Annex Ws and plans to incorporate the template into planning policy. The template does not, however, specifically call attention to the need to plan for the closeout of contracts. Furthermore, in March 2010, we reported that few of the operation plans approved by the Secretary of Defense or his designee even included an Annex W and when they did, those annexes restated broad language from DOD's high-level guidance on operational contract support.[17]

The contracting organizations included in our review generally did not conduct any planning to close the contracts they awarded to support

---

[15] An operation plan describes how DOD will respond to a potential event that might require the use of military force. It is composed of a base plan, which describes the concept of operations, major forces, sustainment concept, and anticipated time lines for completing the mission; and annexes, which provide further details on areas such as intelligence, logistics, personnel, communications, and operational contract support. Chairman of the Joint Chiefs of Staff Manual 3122.03B, *Joint Operation Planning and Execution System (JOPES) Volume II Planning Formats* (Feb. 28, 2006). Superseded by Joint Chiefs of Staff Manual 3122.03C, *Joint Operation Planning and Execution System (JOPES) Volume II Planning Formats* (Aug. 17, 2007).

[16] Joint Chiefs of Staff, Joint Publication 4-10, *Operational Contract Support* (Oct. 17, 2008).

[17] GAO, *Warfighter Support: DOD Needs to Improve Its Planning for Using Contractors to Support Future Military Operations*, GAO-10-472 (Washington, D.C.: Mar. 30, 2010).

operations in Iraq until several years after the contracts were initially awarded. DOD officials noted that the department initially assumed that post-conflict stability and reconstruction efforts would not last for an extended period and as such, any organization that awarded contracts to support these efforts would close contracts under the organization's standard processes. Officials acknowledged that as these efforts continued and the level of contracting activity increased, C3's predecessors attempted to close contracts as time and resources permitted, but did not develop a plan needed to do so. For example,

- The Army did not develop a plan to close its Iraq contracts until 2008, long after reconstruction efforts were underway in Iraq. According to the Army, the 2007 Gansler Commission report's finding that only 5 percent of eligible Iraq contracts were closed prompted the Army to begin planning for and taking steps to address the backlog of over-age Iraq contracts. To do so, in October 2008, the Army established the Task Force and delegated responsibility to DCMA Southern Europe to close a number of C3's cost-type contracts.
- According to USACE personnel, they began focusing on contract closeouts after the Army identified that the Army had more than 660,000 over-age contracts as of January 2009 and established a goal to close all of its over-age contracts by the end of fiscal year 2011. In January 2011, USACE established a contract closeout cell in Winchester, Virginia.
- AFCEE personnel, with 96 over-age Iraq contracts, stated they have not developed an Iraq contract closeout plan and continue to close these contracts as part of their routine contracting activities. AFCEE personnel stated, however, only two contracting personnel are assigned to closing the Iraq contracts and do so only when time and other responsibilities permit.

Commands Focused Limited Staff Resources on Awarding Contracts

DOD officials also noted that the need to focus limited staff resources on fulfilling urgent requirements in support of the war effort, and other contingency-related challenges, contributed to the backlog of contracts to be closed. One senior Army official noted that as there were not enough contracting officers in theater to handle both awards and closeouts, the command focused its attention on awarding contracts. Similarly, C3 and USACE contracting personnel we spoke with stated that they were responsible for awarding, administering, and closing contracts, but to meet urgent requirements, they prioritized contract awards over other activities. In addition, an Army official noted that contracting personnel have little incentive to close contracts, as their success is often measured by contracts awarded. Contracting personnel who are responsible for

GAO-11-891 Contingency Contracting

closing contracts stated, however, that emphasis on timely contract closeout is especially important in a contingency environment because the longer the time from when the contractor completes its work and when the contract is closed, the more difficult it becomes to determine the status of contracts, resolve documentation and administration issues, obtain a release of claims, and negotiate final payments. For example,

- To close a $16.8 million guard services contract, contracting personnel in Iraq described the process of determining how payments were made as "putting together pieces of a puzzle." Personnel stated that they spent several weeks identifying what the contractor billed and was paid by reviewing invoices, contract modifications, and e-mails.
- Similarly, contracting personnel in Iraq stated that resolving an overpayment of over $500,000 has delayed the closeout of another $17 million guard services contract. The contracting officer who awarded and administered the contract was no longer in Iraq when the contracting personnel began closing the contract. These personnel stated that they relied on e-mails in the contract file and obtained payment information from DFAS to determine the extent to which the contractor was overpaid and are awaiting further guidance from DFAS on what steps are needed to recover funds from the contractor.
- Task Force personnel noted that while closing a $1.3 million contract for life support services, they found that there was no documentation in the contract file to explain why services were not performed at three camp sites listed in the contract. The contractor told Task Force personnel that he was instructed not to perform the services but was never provided anything in writing. Task Force personnel noted that the contractor then refused to sign the release of claims, so personnel unilaterally deobligated the remaining funds on the contract to close the contract.
- According to one senior C3 official, contracting officers sometimes relied on documents provided by the contractor to resolve claims because they were not maintained in the contract files. In one instance, while closing a vehicle lease contract, C3 personnel stated that they found 149 damage claims for vehicles, but oversight personnel often did not keep records or pictures of the condition of the vehicles when they were picked up and dropped off by the contractor. The contracting personnel stated that they are coordinating with the payment office and resource managers but said that it may not be possible to locate someone who can verify or dispute the claims.

Task Force personnel stated that they often needed to perform routine contract administration tasks on contracts, including reconciling payments and obligations, acquiring receiving reports, contacting contractors in theater to obtain invoices and release of claims, and piecing together incomplete contract files to provide reasonable assurance that the government received what it paid for and the contract could be closed. Task Force personnel illustrated some of the challenges they often encounter in the following two examples:

- In one case involving the closeout of a $55 million contract for shotguns, goggles, and radios, Task Force personnel stated that they had to reconcile payments against nine different task orders because payments were not made to the correct task orders, including one lump-sum payment for $8 million that did not correspond to any task order, and the contract was missing receiving reports and payment documents. Task Force personnel contacted DFAS to determine how much should have been paid on the task order and verified payments through a data system. Task Force personnel eventually closed all of the task orders between March and December 2010.
- During the closeout of another contract for $101,000 to lease buses from an Iraqi contractor, Task Force personnel found that the contractor was not paid for 1 month of service and not compensated for damages to two of the buses. After contacting DFAS and determining that there were enough funds on the contract to cover the missing payment and repair costs, Task Force personnel notified the payment office to make a final payment to the contractor. Task Force personnel were able to close the contract after the contractor was paid and a release of claims was received.

Workforce Challenges Associated with Transitioning Closeout Responsibilities Have Reduced Capacity to Close Firm-Fixed Price Contracts

C3 has taken steps to reduce the number of firm-fixed price contracts it needs to close, but difficulties with hiring ACC-RI personnel have slowed these efforts. The Army and C3 initially established the Task Force to address the backlog of C3's firm-fixed price contracts awarded before fiscal year 2009 and planned at that time to close any contracts awarded in fiscal year 2009 and later in theater. To ensure the contracts remaining in theater were closed, a senior C3 official established closeout goals in October 2010 and required each regional contracting center to appoint personnel responsible for completing contract closeout. While Army data indicate that progress was made in closing contracts in Iraq, C3 officials told us that closeout goals were tracked informally and acknowledged that some regional contracting centers were unable to meet these goals. By February 2011, the Army changed its strategy and decided that when the Task Force is shut down in September 2011, all C3 contracts, including those awarded after fiscal year 2009, would eventually be transferred to ACC-RI for closeout. According to C3's commanding general, this decision was made because ACC-RI has a workforce that can handle complex contract actions and has expertise in southwest Asia contracting.

By June 2011, the Army had transferred about 15,000 Iraq and Afghanistan contracts awarded between fiscal years 2008 and 2010 from the Task Force to ACC-RI. According to the Army, ACC-RI personnel are in the process of inventorying these contracts and identifying which are closed or require additional administration. Army officials stated that they are reviewing ACC-RI closeout procedures and data collection efforts to ensure Army data are accurate and complete.

During this transition period, ACC-RI has not been able to hire the number of individuals it estimated it needed to manage the anticipated workload and the number of contracts reviewed and closed by the Task Force has fallen considerably. According to Army officials, ACC-RI will need to hire 25 individuals by the time it fully assumes the Task Force's responsibilities. Army officials stated that ACC-RI has experienced challenges hiring contracting personnel in part due to potential applicants' hesitation to accept these positions, which are term positions that expire by October 2012. Army officials stated as of June 2011, ACC-RI had only hired 4 staff but efforts are underway to hire additional personnel. Until these positions can be filled, other ACC-RI personnel are temporarily supporting the closeout efforts. In addition, in July 2011, the ACC-RI issued a task order for contract closeout support to AbilityOne, which provides job opportunities on federal contracts for individuals who are blind or have other disabilities. According to one ACC-RI official, ACC-RI plans to hire nine AbilityOne employees under this contract. It remains uncertain, however, when the Army will be able to review and, as necessary, close the contracts that remain at the Task Force. Similarly, Army officials stated that the Task Force's capacity to close contracts has decreased, as 10 of its 25 staff have resigned in advance of the Task Force's planned closure. During the week of September 3, 2010, the Task Force closed 439 contracts but by the week of June 9, 2011, the Task Force only closed 267 contracts.

Limited DCAA Staffing and Unresolved Contractor Accounting Challenges Hinder Closeout of Cost-Type Contracts

DOD's efforts to close its large, cost-type contracts are hindered by staffing shortages at DCAA and unresolved issues with contractors' cost accounting practices. DOD reported that it had 226 over-age, cost-type Iraq contracts with approximately $19.1 billion in obligations (see table 4). A critical step to closing these contracts is to determine how to allocate a contractor's general administrative and overhead costs to each of its contracts. To do so, DCAA performs annual incurred cost audits on a contractor-by-contractor basis—versus a contract-by-contract basis—by reviewing incurred cost proposals from the contractor for each year of performance. DCAA auditors test direct and indirect costs to determine whether they are allowable, allocable, and reasonable. The direct and indirect costs form the basis for DCAA's recommended indirect cost rate, which is usually used by the contracting officer to negotiate a final rate with the contractor. When the indirect cost rate for the final year of contract performance is settled and the final price of the contract is determined, contract closeout may proceed.

Table 4: Number of DOD Cost-Type Contracts Related to Iraq Eligible for Closeout

Contracting organization	Number of eligible contracts	Number of over-age contracts	Obligations on over-age contracts (in billions of dollars)
ACC-RI LOGCAP	18	17	14.8
C3	109	106	2.6
AFCEE	222	83	1.4
USACE	63	20	0.3
Total	412	226	19.1

Source: GAO analysis of data reported by contracting organizations between January and July of 2011.

DOD's cost-type contracts related to Iraq often spanned multiple years and as such DCAA must complete incurred cost audits for each year of performance. For example, on one contract with performance from 2004 through 2008 and 5 divisions of the contractor claiming costs, DCAA is required to complete 25 audits of costs incurred, one for each year of performance per division. DCAA, however, is still completing audits for this contractor for costs incurred in 2004 and 2005, with audits of the remaining years scheduled for 2011 and after. DCAA officials told us that this condition is due in part to a DCAA-wide shortage of auditors. DCAA data indicates that from fiscal years 2000 to 2011, its workforce grew by 16 percent while DOD research and procurement spending, an indicator of DCAA's workload, increased by 87 percent. In addition, DCAA officials stated that in response to GAO's finding in 2009 on problems with

DCAA's audit quality, including insufficient testing of contractors' support for claimed costs, DCAA now requires more testing and stricter compliance with government auditing standards, which adds to the amount of staff time required to complete each audit.[18] DCAA officials stated that as their workload increased and resources remained relatively constant, auditors prioritized time-sensitive activities, such as audits to support new awards, and incurred cost audits were not completed, creating a backlog.

In planning for its fiscal year 2011 workload requirements, DCAA determined that it had the resources to complete only about half of its entire portfolio of required audits and activities, including both Iraq and non-Iraq work. As a result, DCAA prioritized its high-risk audits, which included the backlog of incurred audits for C3's 106 over-age, cost-type contracts. As of July 2011, DCAA reported that of the 116 incurred cost audits needed to close these C3 contracts, it had completed 27 audits and estimated another 19 audits will be completed by the end of fiscal year 2011. The remaining 70 audits are planned to be completed after fiscal year 2011. DCMA contracting officials responsible for closing C3's cost-type contracts stated that regardless of whether DCAA completes the 19 audits as planned, none of the C3 contracts can be closed by the end of fiscal year 2011 because most of the contractors claimed costs through 2008 or 2009, and the audits will only be completed for costs incurred mostly through 2004 and 2005. Further, there are an additional 31 AFCEE over-age cost-type contracts that will not have final incurred cost audits completed before the end of fiscal year 2011.

To address its resource challenges, DCAA officials reported that it hired over 500 new employees in the past 2 years. DCAA has also requested authority to hire 200 auditors per year over each of the next 5 years. DCAA officials noted, however, that it often takes several years before auditors are properly trained to conduct an incurred cost audit. In addition, in January 2011, DOD issued a memorandum that shifted some audit responsibilities, such as lower dollar price proposal audits and purchasing system reviews, to DCMA to allow DCAA to devote more resources to high-risk work, like the incurred cost audits needed to support the closeout of Iraq contracts. DCAA officials also stated that they plan to

---

[18] GAO, *DCAA Audits: Widespread Problems with Audit Quality Require Significant Reform*, GAO-09-468 (Washington, D.C.: Sept. 23, 2009).

dedicate additional auditors to solely focus on conducting incurred cost audits in fiscal year 2012.

DCAA has identified a number of deficiencies at major defense contractors, which provided support in Iraq, that need to be resolved before the incurred cost audits can be completed. These deficiencies include

- inadequate incurred cost proposals and cost documentation;
- inadequate contractor business systems;
- accounting practices that are not compliant with cost accounting standards,[19] leading to misallocation of costs;
- delays in providing DCAA access to needed records;
- disputes with contractors over unallowable costs; and
- other challenges, such as those due to ongoing litigation.

The following examples illustrate the challenges that DCAA reported for several contractors.

- Due to inadequate incurred cost proposals, DCAA has completed incurred costs audits only through 2003 for one major Iraq contractor that incurred costs through 2010. In total, DOD has $15.3 billion in obligations on over-age, cost-type Iraq contracts awarded to this contractor. DCAA reported that it issued the 2003 incurred cost audit 5 years after the costs were incurred, in part because the contractor repeatedly submitted inadequate incurred cost proposals and did not provide adequate support for costs (see fig. 2). Further, DCAA officials stated that the incurred cost proposals submitted by the contractor for 2004 through 2009 are inadequate but will continue its audits of the 2004 and 2005 proposals.

---

[19] The Cost Accounting Standards are accounting requirements for the measurement, assignment, and allocation of costs to government contracts.

Figure 2: Incurred Cost Audit for One Major Iraq Contractor's 2003 Costs Was Delayed Until 2008 Due in Part to Repeated Inadequate Proposal Submissions

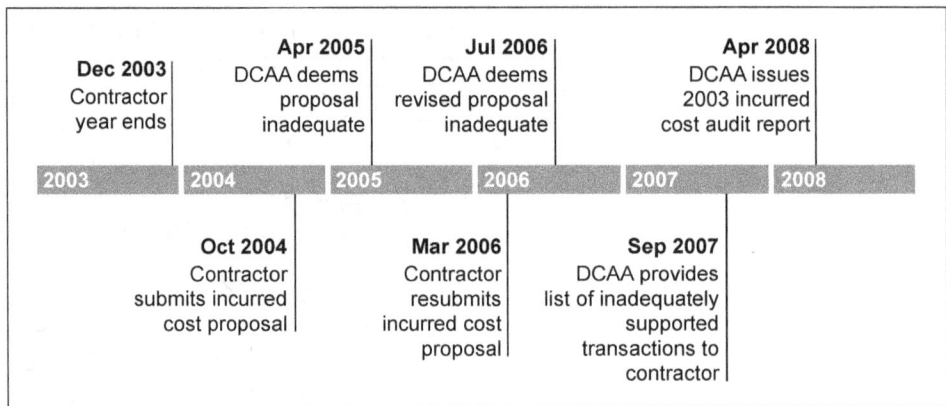

Source: GAO analysis of DCAA's incurred cost audit report.

- Additionally, DCAA reported that this contractor had deficient accounting systems, unresolved issues associated with unallowable costs, noncompliant accounting practices, and legal investigations that further delayed incurred cost audits. In 2006, DCAA reported that the contractor had significant deficiencies in its accounting system that resulted in the contractor charging over $370 million to incorrect task orders from 2002 to 2004, requiring reclassification of costs to the proper task orders. The reclassifications were completed in January 2005. Then, in 2009 and 2010, DCAA found over $185 million in unallowable costs that are pending negotiations with DCMA and settlement of contractor claims. In 2010, DCAA auditors found the contractor did not comply with the cost accounting standard associated with insurance costs, which resulted in an estimated $1.6 million in costs that were misallocated. DCAA reported that the contractor did not respond to DCAA's finding because it had not completed its management review of the allocated costs. Further, according to the auditors, DCAA's incurred cost audit reports could be delayed as the auditors coordinate the issuance of audit reports with various investigative agencies. DCAA auditors do not expect to complete the 2004 and 2005 incurred cost audits for this contractor before the end of fiscal year 2011. In May 2011, the contractor withdrew its 2006 through 2009 incurred cost proposals and stated that it plans to delay its submission of the 2010 incurred cost proposal until November 2011.
- For another major contractor, DCAA identified that the contractor's accounting practices were not compliant with cost accounting

GAO-11-891 Contingency Contracting

standards. DOD has $316 million in obligations on over-age, cost-type Iraq contracts awarded to this contractor with performance between 2004 and 2009. DCAA reported in 2006 that the contractor's accounting practices did not sufficiently remove unallowable costs from a cost proposal, which DCAA auditors stated put additional onus on them to test whether the costs were allowable. In one case, DCAA auditors found the contractor had included over $500,000 in bonuses to senior executives in the incurred cost proposal, even though these costs are expressly unallowable under law. The contractor disagreed with DCAA's findings but agreed to remove these costs from its proposal. As of July 2011, DCAA has completed 5 of the 18 incurred cost audits required to close the contracts.

- DCAA identified deficient subcontract management systems, disputes over unallowable costs, and challenges with access to records as contributing to delays in completing incurred cost audits for another contractor. DOD has $212 million in obligations on over-age, cost-type Iraq contracts awarded to this contractor. In 2005, 2006, and 2009, DCAA auditors reported significant deficiencies in the contractor's subcontract management system that resulted in potential unreasonable and unallowable costs being billed to the government, subcontracts being awarded noncompetitively, and inadequate price analysis. As a result, DCAA auditors had to audit the subcontractors' costs, even though doing so is generally the prime contractor's responsibility. The contractor generally disagreed with DCAA's findings but stated it would evaluate and revise its procedures where necessary to comply with DCAA's recommendations. In addition, in 2010 and 2011, DCAA auditors reported the contractor had over $22.5 million in unallowable subcontract costs, some of which have been appealed by the contractor and some of which are being settled by DCMA. Finally, in 2010, DCAA auditors repeatedly requested but were denied access to support for the 2006 incurred cost proposal, including a $2.3 million procurement file. DCAA reported that its auditors requested the data over a period of 5 months and stated that when the contractor provided the data, they were still inadequate in supporting the claimed costs. DCAA auditors stated as a result, it deemed those costs as unallowable for reimbursement.

DOD has taken steps to address the challenges with auditing contractors' incurred costs. For example, effective June 2011, the FAR was revised to list the minimum information that contractors must include for proposals to be adequate to address the delays resulting from inadequate incurred cost proposals. Also, to improve its oversight of contractor business systems, DOD revised the Defense Federal Acquisition Regulation Supplement in May 2011 to more clearly define contractor business systems, including accounting, estimating, and purchasing, and to allow payments to be withheld from contractors if their business systems contain significant deficiencies.

DOD Has Taken Steps to Mitigate Potential Loss or Misuse of Funds but Limited Visibility into Its Contracts Hinders Such Efforts

DOD has taken steps to identify unspent contract funds and recover improper payments, but limited visibility into its contracts has hindered such efforts. For example, DOD has deobligated some funds to make them available to meet other DOD needs, but there remains at least $135 million that will potentially not be available for use by DOD at the end of fiscal year 2011. DOD generally cannot identify to which contracts these funds are associated. Additionally, instances of improper payments and potential fraud were sometimes found years after final deliveries were made, but contracting personnel may not be able to recover funds owed to the government.

DOD's Efforts to Prioritize the Deobligation of Funds that Will Return to Treasury at the End of the Fiscal Year Are Affected by Poor Visibility into Its Contracts

DOD prioritizes deobligating funds that may potentially be returned to Treasury at the end of each fiscal year so these funds would be available for other DOD uses. DOD contracting organizations, however, have varying degrees of visibility into the amount of funds remaining on their Iraq contracts. Contracting organizations we met with generally could not identify the total and unliquidated obligations associated with their Iraq contracts, in part because the systems used to track contracting information were not linked with systems used to track financial and payment data. Similarly, DOD resource managers, who are responsible for maintaining information on the availability of funding, tracked unspent funds at the appropriation level but did not always have such information on a contract-by-contract basis. DOD estimates that at least $135 million in contract funding could return to Treasury by the end of fiscal year 2011 if not deobligated but there may be additional funds not yet identified (see table 5).

Table 5: Estimated Iraq Contract Funding that Potentially Could Return to Treasury at the End of Fiscal Year 2011

Dollars in millions

Contracting organization	Estimated amount of funds
C3[a]	18.6
AFCEE[b]	unknown
USACE[c]	104.9
ACC-RI LOGCAP[d]	12.3
Total	**135.8**

Source: GAO analysis of DOD data.

[a]Estimates for C3 include both cost-type and firm-fixed price contracts and are as of May and June 2011, respectively.

[b]AFCEE did not track these data for their contracts in theater.

[c]Estimates for USACE are as of March 2011.

[d]Estimates for LOGCAP are as of June 2011.

C3, AFCEE, and USACE contracting organizations generally do not track unspent funds that could be returned to Treasury on a contract-by-contract basis. As a result, resource management personnel stated they are responsible for notifying contracting personnel of these funds. Resource management personnel, however, reported that identifying the appropriate contracting personnel can be time-consuming and labor-intensive, in part because of the rapid turnover of contracting personnel, which often caused the contact information listed in the data systems to be invalid. Contracting personnel stated that once they were aware that funds may be potentially returned to Treasury, they took steps to prioritize deobligating these funds, including checking whether there were pending invoices or claims requiring payments. For example:

C3 did not maintain visibility of unspent funds at the contract level, in part due to limitations in its contracting and financial management systems, but available data indicate that DOD may lose $18.6 million for its use and which will be returned to Treasury at the end of fiscal year 2011. While C3 officials noted that some contracting officers may have tracked unspent funds for contracts for which they were responsible, we found that C3's contracting data systems did not maintain such financial data. After being delegated closeout responsibility for C3's large, cost-type contracts, DCMA Southern Europe undertook efforts to manually track unspent funds on a contract-by-contract basis. DCMA personnel reported that $15.0 million of funds that could be returned to Treasury remained on C3's cost-type contracts as of May 2011, but anticipated having most of these funds deobligated by the end of July 2011. Similarly, without visibility into which firm-fixed price contracts had unspent funds, Task Force personnel focused their efforts on reviewing C3 contracts awarded in fiscal year 2006 to deobligate funds but told us they do not believe they will be able to close all of these contracts before these funds are returned to Treasury. Resource managers at U.S. Army Central—which manages the funds associated with C3's contracts—stated they believe that, as of June 2011, $3.6 million on these contracts will potentially be returned to Treasury.

AFCEE contracting personnel stated that they generally do not maintain visibility into AFCEE's unspent funds at the contract level. For AFCEE's own contracts, contracting personnel generally deobligate funds down to 10 percent of the total obligated amount, or $100,000, whichever is less, to pay for any additional costs that may be identified during DCAA's incurred cost audits. AFCEE contracting personnel reported that for these contracts, they do not believe any funds will be returned to Treasury at the end of fiscal year 2011. AFCEE contracting personnel stated that for the contracts awarded on behalf of other organizations, they are notified by the customers of unspent funds on an ad-hoc basis. AFCEE contracting personnel stated that they prioritize the deobligation of these funds when they are made aware of them, but do not track the total amount of funds that may be returned to Treasury.

USACE contracting personnel stated that they do not maintain information on unspent funds on a contract level, but rather USACE resource managers tracked funds at the account level. For these accounts, USACE resource managers notify contracting personnel, who attempt to identify which contracts are associated with these funds and, as appropriate, take steps to deobligate these funds. USACE reported, however, that $104.9 million have not been deobligated as of March 2011. USACE personnel stated that a majority of these funds are on contracts awaiting DCAA audits.[20]

---

[20] USACE personnel stated that USACE also served as the payment office for a number of contracts awarded by C3 and AFCEE. USACE identified an additional $83.0 million that may potentially return to Treasury at the end of fiscal year 2011 for these contracts as of March 2011. USACE personnel could not identify which contracting offices were responsible for these contracts and is currently coordinating with the Task Force, AFCEE, and DCMA contracting personnel to identify which contracts they have to deobligate these funds.

Conversely, ACC-RI's LOGCAP office tracked funds that could be returned to Treasury on a contract-by-contract basis. ACC-RI contracting personnel stated that they hold weekly meetings with the contractor and resource managers to reconcile financial records and identify funds that could be deobligated. ACC-RI personnel told us that $12.3 million of funds that could be returned to Treasury have not been deobligated as of June 2011, but anticipated having most of these funds deobligated by the end of July 2011.

DOD Incurred Unnecessary Costs because Improper Payments Were Discovered Late

In some instances, DOD discovered improper payments during the contract closeout process years after the contractors delivered the final good or service, but some attempts to recover overpayments were unsuccessful and, at times, late payments to contractors resulted in interest fees.[21] According to DFAS personnel responsible for recovering overpayments made on some Iraq contracts, if contracts were closed immediately after final payments are made, overpayments could be discovered earlier, which increases the likelihood of recovering payments. For example, when the contractor is still conducting business with the government, DFAS can reduce payments on one contract to offset overpayments made on another contract. Task Force personnel noted that for a 2005 vehicle lease contract, contracting personnel in theater found the contractor was overpaid by over $41,000 on several invoices and subsequently DFAS withheld payments on several of the contractor's other contracts to completely offset the overpayment. DFAS personnel, however, stated that the more time that has passed from when the contractor was mistakenly paid, the more difficult it becomes to recover those payments because the contractor may no longer be in business with the U.S. government or may have changed address or name. In several instances, overpayments on contracts for goods or services delivered in 2007 or earlier were not referred to DFAS until 2010 (see

---

[21] Improper payments are defined as any payment that should not have been made or that was made in an incorrect amount (including overpayments and underpayments) under statutory, contractual, administrative, or other legally applicable requirements. It also includes any payment to an ineligible recipient or ineligible service, duplicate payments, payments for services not received, and any payment for an incorrect amount. In 2009, GAO reported that DOD's processes to conduct risk assessments, estimate improper payments, and develop corrective actions to reduce improper payments had significant weaknesses. See GAO, *Improper Payments: Significant Improvements Needed in DOD's Efforts to Address Improper Payment and Recovery Auditing Requirements*, GAO-09-442 (Washington, D.C.: July 29, 2009).

table 6). DFAS personnel stated that in these cases, despite numerous attempts to contact the contractor, they have yet to recover the overpayments. As of June 2011, two of the contracts have been referred to Treasury and one contract has been referred to another DFAS office for further debt collection efforts.

Table 6: Examples of Contracts with Overpayments that Were Not Recovered

Description of contract good or service	Delivery date	Date referred to DFAS	Amount of unrecovered overpayment
Gymnasium	10/8/2004	8/18/2010	$104,696
Linguist building construction	3/11/2007	9/27/2010	$170,000
Latrines with servicing	10/31/2007	10/5/2010	$27,200

Source: GAO analysis of Task Force and DFAS data.

In a few instances, Task Force personnel did not refer overpayments to DFAS because they determined the excess payments were relatively small in value or unlikely to be recovered. For example, Task Force personnel found that the U.S. government overpaid a contractor by $8,100 for trash services provided in 2006 and 2007. After unsuccessful attempts to contact the contractor, Task Force personnel closed the contract in 2009, noting that so much time had passed since the final payment that it was unreasonable to expect that the overpayment could be recovered.

C3 is unable to mitigate the amount of interest payments that may be associated with late payments because the contracting and financial management systems cannot identify which contracts still require payment, especially for contracts awarded between 2003 and 2007. Task Force personnel stated that given the limitations of these systems, they must review the contract file to determine whether a contract requires additional payment. For example, while closing a $94,500 contract for vehicle lease services in Iraq, Task Force personnel discovered the contractor may not have been paid for 2 months' worth of vehicle lease services, so the Task Force is attempting to contact personnel in theater to confirm whether services were rendered. Additionally, some contracts requiring final payments were not paid until years after the final delivery, which resulted in interest payments. DFAS personnel reported that DFAS has paid $2.8 million in interest payments on Iraq contracts as of June 2011, though it is not possible to determine the amount of interest payments associated with over-age contracts.

DOD took steps to improve its payment processes in Iraq, but some challenges with timely payments remain. According to DFAS officials, in 2008, DFAS became responsible for making payments for contracts awarded in theater with obligations of $25,000 or more and in 2010 DFAS and C3 agreed to lower this threshold to $3,000. DFAS officials stated this decision was made to improve internal controls by ensuring that adequate documentation was available before payments are made in theater. DFAS officials noted, however, there were some payment delays because payment documentation requirements were not always met. One C3 official noted that these payment processing delays led to some Iraqi vendors being unwilling to do business with the U.S. government and walking off job sites. C3's commanding general stated that when contracts are not closed out and vendors have not been paid for goods and services that they provided to the U.S. government, this contributes to negative perceptions about Americans.

Finally, late contract closeouts may hinder efforts to identify and address potential fraud found on the C3 contracts because they were reported to investigators years after the potential fraudulent activities took place and the contract files were poorly maintained. As Task Force personnel reviewed and closed C3 contracts, they identified 151 contracts with potential fraudulent activities and referred these contracts to the Army's Criminal Investigations Division. For example, in one contract for a cable fiber network, Task Force personnel stated that they found evidence that the contracting officer had made a payment of $84,000 in cash, but the contractor's invoice was only for $64,000. There was no documentation in the file to account for the $20,000 difference between the disbursement and invoice, so Task Force personnel referred this case to the Army's criminal investigators. According to an Army investigator, it was difficult to determine whether this case and other cases were due to fraudulent activity or contracting errors, in part because the contracts did not have enough documentation to build a case. Furthermore, the Army investigator stated that many of the referred contracts had been awarded many years ago so following up on these cases has been challenging, as many of the contracting personnel and contractors involved are no longer available.

Growing Backlog of Afghanistan Contracts Suggests Problems Related to Closing Contracts Will Continue

DOD reported that actions are underway to address the lessons learned in Iraq, including developing deployable contract management systems and explicitly requiring that contract closeout requirements be incorporated into contingency contracting planning documents. DOD officials acknowledge, however, they are likely to face similar problems with closing contracts awarded to support efforts in Afghanistan. For example, the backlog of C3's Afghanistan contracts that need to be closed is growing steadily, but the Army's capacity to close these contracts in the United States remains in question due to challenges with transitioning closeout responsibilities from the Task Force to ACC-RI.

DOD Has Identified and Addressed Some of the Problems Associated with Closing Iraq Contracts

In October 2010, as part of the Army's Operational Contract Support Lessons Learned Program, C3 identified lessons learned from contracting in Iraq between 2005 and 2010. As part of this effort, C3 identified the need to improve and consolidate data management, improve contract oversight, and increase emphasis on contract administration and closeout. DOD officials told us they had already implemented or planned new practices, as the following examples illustrate.

- C3 officials noted that they had implemented the Standard Procurement System in both Iraq and Afghanistan to better document information on contracts awarded during and after fiscal year 2009 and have worked to improve the data input into the system. Defense Procurement and Acquisition Policy officials and a representative from the Joint Chiefs of Staff told us they are also identifying and developing deployable contract writing and management systems with the intent that one day contingency contracting personnel will use the same contract management tools in theater that are used in the United States.
- C3 also identified that contract oversight was a historic problem and noted the need to ensure contracting officer's representatives fulfilled their oversight responsibilities. In March 2010, the Under Secretary of Defense for Acquisition, Technology and Logistics issued new certification requirements for contracting officer's representatives to ensure they are experienced and trained before they are appointed to oversee contractor performance. In June 2011, we reported, however,

that DOD personnel in Afghanistan were not always fully prepared for their roles and responsibilities to provide adequate oversight there.[22]

- Defense Procurement and Acquisition Policy has also issued and since updated the Defense Contingency Contracting Handbook, which includes reference material to ensure contingency contracting officers maintain proper contract documentation and complete closeout duties. For example, the handbook includes guidance on the essential documents that should be in a contract file, identifies steps to ensure contracts are properly enumerated to avoid duplicate contract numbers, and recognizes the need to close contracts as soon as possible.

Finally, DOD is in the process of determining how it will address the problems C3 attributed to a lack of planning for the contracting requirements in Iraq. A senior C3 official recommended that operational campaign plans include a contracting annex, such as an Annex W. In such cases when an Annex W would be required, we found that Joint Publication 4-10 and DOD's Annex W guidance do not fully address the need to plan for contract closeout requirements—including identifying responsibilities, either in or outside of theater, for closing contracts. United States Forces-Iraq issued an Annex W in 2011, which included directions for personnel to take steps to close contracts in Iraq, well after C3's backlog of contracts was identified. Representatives from the Joint Chiefs of Staff responsible for revising Joint Publication 4-10 and the Annex W guidance recognize the need to incorporate more specific language on the need to plan for contract closeout during the contingency contracting planning process. These officials stated that they plan to issue new Annex W guidance by the end of 2011 and intend to add more specific language regarding contract closeout.

Steadily Increasing Backlog of C3's Afghanistan Contracts Suggests Closeout Problems May Persist

As was the case in Iraq, C3 officials stated that prior to the build-up of forces in Afghanistan, contract closeout was a challenge because there were not enough contracting personnel in theater to meet competing contracting demands. To address its backlog of contracts awarded before fiscal year 2009, C3 delegated responsibility for closing at least 22,597 Afghanistan inactive contracts to the Task Force.[23] Task Force

---

[22] GAO, *Operational Contract Support: Actions Needed to Address Contract Oversight and Vetting of Non-U.S. Vendors in Afghanistan*, GAO-11-771T (Washington, D.C.: June 30, 2011).

[23] We could not identify the place of performance for over 14,000 other contracts that were sent to the Task Force to be closed.

data indicate that 3,510, or about 16 percent, of these contracts have been reviewed as of April 2011. Task Force personnel stated that they faced the same challenges with closing the Afghanistan contracts as those associated with the Iraq contracts, such as poor contract documentation and improper payments.

According to C3's commanding general and senior contracting officials, these challenges were exacerbated during the build-up of U.S. military personnel in Afghanistan, and the focus remains on meeting the warfighter's needs. C3 officials told us the number of contracting officers in Afghanistan increased from about 60 in 2008 to about 200 in April 2011. In part, this increase in personnel enabled C3 to close over 18,600 contracts awarded between fiscal years 2009 and 2011. Despite these efforts, however, the number of contracts eligible to be closed continues to grow. For example, as of April 2008, C3 data indicated that 1,471 Afghanistan contracts remained in theater that were eligible but over age for closeout. As of May 2011, the number of contracts eligible but over age for closeout has increased to over 16,900 contracts. Additionally, C3 will have to close over 7,000 other contracts awarded during this period that are eligible but not yet over age for closeout. C3 officials told us they expect that more Afghanistan contracts will be transferred out of theater to be closed by ACC-RI, likely after much of the remaining Iraq contracts are closed. As previously noted, however, the Army's ability to close contracts remains in question due to challenges with transitioning closeout responsibilities to ACC-RI.

Conclusions

Contract closeout is a key step to ensure the government receives the goods and services it purchases at the agreed upon price and, if done in a timely manner, provides opportunities to utilize unspent funds for other DOD needs. In Iraq, however, contract closeout was often an afterthought or was done as time permitted. The complications DOD has faced with closing its Iraq contracts underscore the importance of advanced planning to close contracts awarded in a contingency environment, encouraging a greater command emphasis on completing and overseeing administrative requirements, establishing a process to provide better management visibility and insight into contracting efforts, and ensuring that DOD's contracting workforce has the capacity to provide appropriate contract administration and contractor oversight. Meeting warfighter needs is paramount, but doing so does not lessen the need to ensure that contracts are properly administered and executed.

DOD's recognition in 2008 that it needed to address the backlog of contracts that are over age for closeout and its establishment of the Task Force came too late in the operation to make a significant difference in closing contracts within the required time frames. By not fully understanding the scope of the backlog and waiting to address it, DOD underestimated the efforts required to close these contracts. Further, the limited visibility provided by the contracting and financial management systems hindered DOD's ability to identify and address improper payments. Challenges with transitioning closeout responsibilities to ACC-RI appear to have hindered the progress the Army had made in closing its Iraq contracts. With over 100,000 C3 Iraq and Afghanistan contracts that need to be reviewed and closed, as appropriate, further delays in closing these contracts can be expected. Finally, closing the large cost-type contracts is further hindered by DCAA's shortage of auditors and problems with contractor accounting practices. DOD has recognized the need to increase DCAA's staffing and address contractor business systems, but fully implementing these initiatives will take several years.

Recommendations for Executive Action

To help address the current backlog of contracts supporting the efforts in Iraq and Afghanistan that need to be closed out, we recommend that the Secretary of Defense direct the Secretary of the Army to take steps to ensure ACC-RI's planned resources are adequate to meet forecasted closeout demands.

To help improve DOD's ability to manage the closeout of contracts awarded in support of future contingencies, we recommend that the Secretary of Defense, in coordination with the Chairman of the Joint Chiefs of Staff, take the following two actions:

- revise DOD's contingency contracting doctrine and guidance to reflect the need for advanced planning for contract closeout; and
- require senior contracting officials to monitor and assess the progress of contract closeout activities throughout the contingency operation so steps may be taken if a backlog emerges.

Agency Comments and Our Evaluation

DOD provided written comments on a draft of this report. DOD concurred with the three recommendations and identified a number of ongoing and planned actions to address them. For example, DOD noted that Army Contracting Command-Rock Island will utilize contractors and explore additional options, such as the Wounded Warrior program, to assist in closing contracts. DOD also noted that it recently amended the Defense

Federal Acquisition Regulation Supplement and provided additional guidance to DOD personnel to underscore the need to understand the unique requirements and considerations associated with planning and executing contingency contract administration services in contingency operations. DOD also plans to further revise its guidance to address the need for contracting officers to do advance planning for closeout of contracts performed in contingency areas. DOD also indicated it intends to issue a revised Joint Publication 4-10, its contingency contracting planning doctrine, in June 2012 to reflect the need for such planning. DOD also provided technical comments, which were incorporated as appropriate. DOD's comments are reprinted in appendix II.

We are sending copies of this report to the Secretary of Defense, the Secretaries of the Army and Air Force; the Under Secretary of Defense (Acquisition, Technology, and Logistics); the Director, Defense Procurement and Acquisition Policy; the Under Secretary of Defense (Comptroller) and Chief Financial Officer; the Chairman, Joint Chiefs of Staff; the Commander, U.S. Central Command; the Director, Defense Contract Audit Agency; the Director, Defense Finance and Accounting Service; and interested congressional committees. In addition, the report will be made available at no charge on GAO's Web site at http://www.gao.gov.

If you or your staff have any questions concerning this report, please contact me at (202) 512-4841. Contact points for our Offices of Congressional Relations and Public Affairs may be found on the last page of this report. GAO staff who made major contributions to this report are listed in appendix III.

John P. Hutton
Director
Acquisition and Sourcing Management

List of Addressees

The Honorable Carl Levin
Chairman
The Honorable John McCain
Ranking Member
Committee on Armed Services
United States Senate

The Honorable Joseph I. Lieberman
Chairman
Committee on Homeland Security and Governmental Affairs
United States Senate

The Honorable Claire McCaskill
Chairman
Ad Hoc Subcommittee on Contracting Oversight
Committee on Homeland Security and Governmental Affairs
United States Senate

The Honorable Howard P. McKeon
Chairman
The Honorable Adam Smith
Ranking Member
Committee on Armed Services
House of Representatives

Appendix I: Scope and Methodology

To assess the Department of Defense's (DOD) efforts to close its Iraq contracts, under the authority of the Comptroller General to conduct evaluations on his own initiative, we examined the (1) total number of its contracts with performance in Iraq that are eligible for closeout and the extent to which DOD closed these contracts within required time frames, (2) factors that contributed to contracts not being closed within required time frames, (3) steps DOD took to manage the financial risks associated with not closing contracts within required time frames, and (4) how DOD captured and implemented lessons learned from closing its Iraq contracts.

To determine the number and value of DOD's Iraq contracts eligible for closeout and the extent to which DOD will close these contracts within required time frames, we reviewed the Federal Acquisition Regulation (FAR) and the Defense Federal Acquisition Regulation Supplement which provide the time frames and the procedures for closing contracts. For the purpose of our review the term contracts refers to all base contracts, task orders, and blanket purchase agreement call orders. We obtained contract data from four DOD organizations which our prior work indicated had been responsible for awarding the majority of contracts with performance in Iraq: CENTCOM Contracting Command (C3), Army Contracting Command-Rock Island (ACC-RI), US Army Corps of Engineers (USACE), and Air Force Center for Engineering and the Environment. These organizations may retain responsibility for administering and closing the contracts they awarded, or may they may delegate such responsibilities to another organization. In those instances, we obtained contract data from that organization, which includes Defense Contract Management Agency, ACC-RI, and C3's Contract Closeout Task Force Office (Task Force). From each organization, we requested the following data for contracts for which they are responsible: contract and order numbers, period of performance, contract type, contract status, total obligations, total unliquidated obligations, and physical completion dates. We identified contracts that were eligible for closeout and over age for closeout based on the time frames established in the FAR. We also identified contracts that did not have complete data to determine eligibility for closeout, but we determined these contracts to be eligible and over age according to data available. We assessed the reliability of these data reported by the contracting organizations through interviews with knowledgeable officials and electronic data testing for missing data, outliers, and obvious errors within each database. While we found that C3's contract data from fiscal years 2003 through 2008 were generally unreliable for determining the closeout status of contracts, they were sufficiently reliable for determining the minimum number of contracts awarded during this time period. We did not evaluate or assess the reliability of the financial management systems used to provide financial data for the purpose of our review. We also did not independently evaluate whether DOD closed individual contracts in accordance with the procedures outlined in the FAR or other DOD guidance.

To identify the factors that contributed to contracts not being closed within FAR-required time frames, we analyzed data provided by and interviewed officials at each of the contracting organizations and the Defense Finance and Accounting Service (DFAS), which is responsible for making payments on some of the Iraq contracts. To understand any challenges faced by DOD contracting personnel in closing individual contracts, we reviewed contract documents for 25 firm-fixed price contracts purposefully selected to obtain a variety of closeout organizations and a range of closeout difficulty and interviewed contracting personnel on their experiences with closing them. We also reviewed Task Force and ACC-RI closeout data to assess the Army's ability to close C3's contracts. In addition, to identify the factors that affected the closeout of cost-type contracts, we interviewed personnel at each of the contracting organizations. In addition, we purposefully selected eight contractors with varying amounts of over-age cost-type contracts, obligations on contracts, and remaining unliquidated obligations and reviewed DCAA's incurred cost and other audit reports for these contracts, and interviewed DCAA officials at headquarters and eight field offices to determine the factors affected their ability to complete the audits. We also reviewed Joint Publication 4-10; the Defense Contingency Contracting Handbook; and the Defense Contract Management Agency's contract closeout guidance and handbook to assess the guidance provided to DOD contracting personnel regarding the need to plan the contract closeout process.

To determine the steps DOD has taken to manage the financial risks associated with not closing contracts within FAR time frames, we reviewed the DOD Financial Management Regulation and each contracting office's closeout guidance. We also interviewed contracting and financial management personnel at the Office of the Under Secretary of Defense, Comptroller; Office of the Assistant Secretary of the Army, Financial Management & Comptroller; U.S. Forces – Iraq, Force Structure Resources and Assessment (J-8); U.S. Army Central Command; and USACE. In addition, we analyzed unliquidated obligation data provided by both the contracting personnel and financial management personnel to determine how these funds were managed. To determine the steps DOD has taken to manage other risks of not closing contracts timely, we reviewed data and interviewed officials from C3; the Task Force; DFAS, which is responsible for collecting overpayments and tracking interest payments; and the Army's Criminal Investigations Division, which is responsible for investigating instances of fraudulent activity found in contracts.

To assess the extent to which DOD captured and implemented lessons learned from closing contracts in contingency operations, we interviewed contracting officials at each of the organizations we visited to identify any lessons learned and reviewed documentation when available. We also interviewed senior contracting officials in Iraq and Afghanistan to identify any changes made in response to the lessons learned from closing the C3 contracts. We reviewed DOD's current contingency contracting doctrine and guidance, and interviewed officials from the Joint Chiefs of Staff who are responsible for revising the doctrine and guidance. We also interviewed officials from the Office of Under Secretary of Defense for Acquisition, Technology, and Logistics' Office of Defense Procurement and Acquisition Policy and the Office of the Deputy Assistant Secretary for the Army (Procurement) to identify any policy changes that may result from the lessons learned in Iraq. We obtained and reviewed C3 data on the total number of its Afghanistan contracts eligible and over age for closeout to assess its ability to close these contracts.

We conducted this performance audit from July 2010 through September 2011 in accordance with generally accepted government auditing standards. Those standards require that we plan and perform the audit to obtain sufficient, appropriate evidence to provide a reasonable basis for our findings and conclusions based on our audit objectives. We believe that the evidence obtained provides a reasonable basis for our findings and conclusions based on our audit objectives.

Appendix II: Comments from the Department of Defense

OFFICE OF THE UNDER SECRETARY OF DEFENSE
3000 DEFENSE PENTAGON
WASHINGTON. DC 20301-3000

ACQUISITION.
TECHNOLOGY
AND LOGISTICS

Mr. John T. Hutton   SEP 2 6 2011
Director, Acquisition and Sourcing Management
U.S. Government Accountability Office
441 G Street, N.W.
Washington, DC 20548

Dear Mr. Hutton:

This is the Department of Defense (DoD) response to the GAO draft report 11-891, "CONTINGENCY CONTRACTING: Improved Planning and Management Oversight Needed to Address Challenges in Closing Contracts," dated August 23, 2011 (GAO Code 120931). Detailed comments on the report recommendations are enclosed. Technical comments were provided separately for your consideration.

The Department appreciates the opportunity to comment on the draft report. My point of contact for this effort is Mr. Bill Reich, william.reich@osd.mil, 571-256-7009.

Sincerely,

Richard Ginman
Director, Defense Procurement
and Acquisition Policy

Enclosure:
As stated

GAO Draft Report Dated August 23, 2011
GAO-11-891 (GAO CODE 120931)

"GAO Draft Report, GAO-11-891, "CONTINGENCY CONTRACTING:
Improved Planning and Management Oversight Needed to Address
Challenges with Closing Contracts," dated August 23, 2011 (GAO Code
120931)

DEPARTMENT OF DEFENSE COMMENTS
TO THE GAO RECOMMENDATIONS

RECOMMENDATION 1: The GAO recommends that the Secretary of Defense direct the
Secretary of the Army to take steps to ensure Army Contracting Command-Rock Island's
(ACC-RI) planned resources are adequate to meet forecasted closeout demands.

DOD RESPONSE: Concur with comment. C-JTSCC, in coordination with ACC-RI, will
provide contract closeout data on a quarterly basis in order for the Deputy Assistant Secretary of
the Army (DASA(P)) to meet the recommendation to ensure resources are adequate to meet
forecasted closeout demands. The availability of ACC-RI rotational personnel was effectively
leveraged to start work despite delays with hiring term personnel. Due to the availability of
ACC-RI rotational personnel, ACC-RI was able to make progress in closing contracts while
striving towards hiring dedicated ACC-RI closeout personnel. Additionally, ACC-RI issued a
Task Order under an existing contract for six closeout specialists, a supervisor and two
warehouse personnel. Funding was provided by DASA(P). The ACC-RI also identified the
Wounded Warrior program as a potential source of personnel. The ACC-RI will begin to utilize
hiring flexibilities available under their authority. To assist ACC-RI, DASA(P) began
recruitment actions for ACC-RI in the beginning of FY11. To date, three people from the
Contract Closeout Task Force Office (CCTFO) have accepted offers and will relocate to ACC-RI
after CCTFO drawdown 30 September 2011. Five additional personnel were hired from a list of
qualified applicants provided to ACC-RI by the DASA(P). They reported in late June 2011.

RECOMMENDATION 2: The GAO recommends that the Secretary of Defense revise DoD's
contingency contracting doctrine and guidance to reflect the need for advanced planning for
contract closeout.

DOD RESPONSE: Concur. Joint Publication (JP) 4-10 is in the process of being updated by
the Joint Staff J-4, Logistics Directorate. The Joint Staff Doctrine Sponsor and lead agent for
this update have agreed to add this planning consideration to the revised publication, which is
expected to be released by June 2012. The need to understand the unique requirements and
considerations associated with planning and executing contingency contract administration
services (CCAS) in contingency operations was recently added to Defense Federal Acquisition
Regulation Supplement and Procedures, Guidance, and Information (DFARS PGI) at
207.105(b)(20)(C)(8) and 225.7404. Draft DFARS PGI language is also being developed that
addresses the need for contracting officers to do advance planning for closeout of contracts
performed in contingency areas.

RECOMMENDATION 3: The GAO recommends that the Secretary of Defense require senior contracting officials to monitor and assess the progress of contract closeout activities throughout the contingency operation so steps may be taken if a backlog emerges.

DOD RESPONSE: Concur. C-JTSCC is monitoring and assessing the progress of contract closeout activities in Iraq and Afghanistan by identifying candidate contract closeouts through the Army Contracting Business Intelligence System (ACBIS) database and weekly updates from ACC-RI. Draft DFARS and PGI language is being developed that addresses this contract closeout requirements and contract administration in support of contingency operations. For future contingency operations, this recommendation will be addressed in the JP 4-10 update.

Appendix III: GAO Contact and Staff Acknowledgments

GAO Contact	John P. Hutton, (202) 512-4841 or huttonj@gao.gov
Acknowledgments	In addition to the individual named above key contributors to this report were Timothy DiNapoli, Assistant Director; Johana Ayers; Noah Bleicher; Seth Carlson; Morgan Delaney-Ramaker; Justin Jaynes; Julia Kennon; John Krump; Claire Li; Anne McDonough-Hughes; and Roxanna Sun.

www.ingramcontent.com/pod-product-compliance
Lightning Source LLC
Chambersburg PA
CBHW080621290526
45790CB00007B/2870